Love,

Grandmother's
FENG SHUI
WISDOM

Grandmother's FENG SHUI WISDOM

TEACHING THE DRAGON WAYS

CHANTAL MONTÉ

CONARI PRESS

First published in 2006 by
Red Wheel/Weiser, LLC
York Beach, ME
With offices at:
500 Third St., Suite 230
San Francisco, CA 94107
www.redwheelweiser.com

Library of Congress Cataloging-in-Publication Data
Monté, Chantal. Grandmother's feng shui wisdom : teaching the dragon ways / Chantal Monte.
p. cm.
ISBN 1-57863-373-7 (alk. paper)
1. Feng shui. I. Title.
BF1779.F4M66 2006
133.3'337—dc22
2005030460

13 12 11 10 09 08 07 06
8 7 6 5 4 3 2 1

Typeset in Hiroshige and Papyrus by Suzanne Albertson
Printed in Canada
FR

To my Grandmother,
for all that she was
and still is

ACKNOWLEDGMENTS

Many thank yous to:

Ann Rafferty, the designer, for instilling your beauty,
grace, and heart throughout this book.

My mother for the gift of life.

My Aunt Nina for your eternal love and support.

And Anthony, my love, my heart.

FOREWORD

Chantal Monté learned the ancient art of feng shui at the knee of her beloved grandmother, who was raised in Jakarta, Indonesia, with a deep belief in Asian traditions, ceremonies, and superstitions as well as classical training in "the art of placement."

Chantal learned how to properly arrange the rooms in her home, but also how to live and breath the tenets of feng shui in every area of her life. As a feng shui consultant, designer, and writer, Chantal allows her innate creativity to infuse every chair, chop stick, broken plate, body and soul that enters her world. She can find the flow of a home and guide it into prosperity and peace. It is these ancient harmonies of living that are channeled through her grandmother and finally to you.

Chantal imparts her grandmother's wisdom through simply and beautifully designed words that echo the original intent of this ancient Chinese system, which was to live in harmony with the natural elements and the earth's forces. *Grandmother's Feng Shui Wisdom* does not tell you how to live, but rather shows you how to live better. Suddenly there is meaning and energy in the way a chop stick is laid across a bowl or a sudden spray of spilled sugar flying across a table top. Every object, its placement and positioning, has significance, a secret life intertwined with yours. Through brief, haiku-like snatches of grandmotherly knowledge, Chantal illuminates the manifestations of unseen forces in the natural world, opening the spiritual realm of gods and charms and lucky spirits to any eyes willing to see it.

Some of Chantal's sayings are charming, sweet and old worldly—just the kind of words that spring from ancient tongues, telling you to watch out, to be careful, to know the deeper meanings of things. Others contain folksy wisdom that cannot be denied, but is too often ignored. Some of Chantal's gems plunge directly into the hectic buzz of modern life and instill a deep sense of calm. It is the combination of all these things that creates a core of serenity, wit and focus to *Grandmother's Feng Shui Wisdom,* giving it a unique voice that stands alone among a plethora of feng shui texts. *Grandmother's Feng Shui Wisdom* shows you the way of the dragon, the way of the ancients, and the way of your grandmother, who always knows best.

Damian Sharp
author of *Simple Feng Shui* and
Learning Astrology
San Francisco, CA

INTRODUCTION

My grandmother raised me in
the ancient and powerful
tradition of Feng Shui.
Not as an art, but as a natural
way of balancing the everyday
aspects of life.

Not too strong, not too weak
or there will be a problem!

To her it was a way to live, treat
one another, succeed, overcome
difficulties, and to be a good
person.

She lived it.
She breathed it.
She played with it.

She taught me to rub Buddha's
belly and to trust in the powerful
intentions of the simplest
rituals.

The sayings in this book come
straight from her heart,
through me to you!

Cease seeing with the
mind and see with the
vital spirit.

Chuang Tzu

When you have company over,
don't let everyone
leave the house at once;
too much energy will
be taken out.

Don't cut hair or nails at
night or you will
call in the spirits.

(Sometimes I felt she was being
silly or overly superstitious.)

Don't cut or sew on your
body because it
symbolizes surgery.

Negative things come in
threes. Positive
things come in twos.

If you have a dream where
you are missing your teeth
or hair, cut a small piece
of hair and flush it
down the toilet to avoid
becoming ill.

If there is a ghost in the house,
ask its name;
if it doesn't say it,
ask it to leave.

(Other times I delighted in the
practical wisdom she applied
to the unseen.)

Writing a person's name on a
piece of paper and putting it
in the freezer will help end
the relationship.

Single woman:
Wear a ring on your
right index finger and you will
meet a man within three
months.

To ensure engagement,
wear the ring on your
right middle finger.

Old Chinese secret

Married woman:
To ensure a good
marriage, wear a ring on
both ring fingers.

™

Don't show off—you'll
use it all up.

To avoid homesickness,
carry some water and soil
from your old house to
your new house;
disperse them in the garden.

Laying chopsticks across
your bowl stops the chi
of Heaven from going
into the bowl.

(There was a heightened focus to my
grandmother's way of seeing
things, so that the simplest
everyday item had an energy of its
own and required attention and respect!)

When cooking, don't hit
utensils against the pan
as this will change the
energy of the food.

When you take away
from the earth, you have to
give back.

Do not celebrate a
birthday early or you will
be tempting fate.

When you drop or spill
something, instead of
getting upset
lie down next to it.

Don't whistle at night
or you will call in
bad spirits.

(Now I understand the powerful
energies of the five elements—wood,
water, fire, earth, and metal—but
when I was little I thought she just
wanted peace and quiet at night.)

If you spill sugar, it
signifies an upcoming wedding.

(I came to see that the simplest of
things are manifestations of
energies and unseen forces, and have
an influence all their own.)

Move twenty-seven things in your
home
and your life will
change.

Old Chinese proverb

天王教菩薩見

If you place money
under Buddha,
he will make it grow.
(And don't forget to
rub his belly!)

HEAVEN BANK NOTE
No. 168168
ONE THOUSAND
1000

On New Year's Eve,
turn on all the lights in
the house and wear all
your money on your body.
Then you will always
have enough to live on
and always have what
you need.

Throwing rice at a new
couple feeds the evil
spirits and distracts
them, keeping the new
marriage safe.

(To my grandmother, a handful of
rice was more potent than
therapists, lawyers, armies of
soldiers, or even chicken soup!)

45

The first time you are invited
to a house,
ask for a second helping of rice
to ensure getting invited back.

Smoke and sound
connect to the other
realms.

(Things are not always what they seem.)

Flowers are Spirit made
manifest.

.

Eat all your rice or you'll
never be rich.

(A daily mantra from my grandmother
at dinnertime. I was known for never
finishing all the food on my plate.
I creatively explained that I was offering
food to the Gods—I don't think
she bought it. Eventually, I came
to realize that she wanted me
to be aware of how fortunate we were.
And to this day, the Gods, my
family, and I all eat very well.)

Here's a ritual for clearing the house and body—best performed the evening before the full moon or the last day of the month:

Open the front and back doors of your
home.

Near the front or back door,
place the following items
on a small table:
metal bowl
a stack of joss paper (easily found at an Asian market)
a bowl of uncooked rice
incense
water and
fruit offerings.

Let the incense burn for 5-10
minutes and set your intentions.
Throw the rice in four
directions over your head, starting
from the north and ending with
the west. Sprinkle the water in a
similar fashion.

Burn the joss paper completely.
Let the smoke enter the house.
Step over the fire of joss paper three times
to clear your body.
Place the cool ashes
in your yard.
(Everything goes back to the earth.)

Rice, water, and the sweet
smell of incense induce the
Gods to listen to your prayers.

Burning the joss paper clears
negativity from the house;
stepping over the fire three
times removes negativity from
your body.

To clear old energies or
renew energies for your
Deity or Statue:
place it outside on a sunny day.
The sun will clear it.

Place Statues or Deities higher
than your waist, if possible, and
especially never touching the floor,
in respect for their higher
energies.

Recipe for a Rice Offering

Cook one cup of jasmine rice.
Let stand and cool.
Reheat rice with:
⅛ cup sweetened condensed milk
(you may add whole milk to desired texture)
2 tsp. Cardamom
1 tsp. Cinnamon

In Feng Shui everything is alive!

To honor your Deities, serve them this offering.
They will take its essence.
This will keep them happy and balanced.
They will take its essence as they miss our earthly delights.
You may consume the rice the next day.

ABOUT THE AUTHOR

Chantal Monté grew up in the San Francisco Bay Area in a household where Eastern beliefs and ancient traditions were practiced daily. Her personal style and various interests reflect the traditional wisdom passed down to her by her Indonesian grandmother. Chantal is certified in the Feng Shui arts, Reiki, Theta Healing, and Ayurvedic Beauty, and furthers her life studies by studying with renowned holistic teachers from around the world. MATJAN, a company formed and run by Chantal and her husband, produces life-enhancing products to balance and expand one's awareness of self and the environment. Please visit *www.chantalmonte.com* and *www.matjandesign.com* and for more information.

love,
Chantal

TO OUR READERS

Weiser Books, an imprint of Red Wheel/Weiser, publishes books across the entire spectrum of occult and esoteric subjects. Our mission is to publish quality books that will make a difference in people's lives without advocating any one particular path or field of study. We value the integrity, originality, and depth of knowledge of our authors.

Our readers are our most important resource, and we appreciate your input, suggestions, and ideas about what you would like to see published. Please feel free to contact us, to request our latest book catalog, or to be added to our mailing list.

Red Wheel/Weiser, LLC
P.O. Box 612
York Beach, ME 03910-0612
www.redwheelweiser.com

般若波羅蜜經

觀世音菩薩

一心稱名觀世音菩薩

念彼觀音力

百千萬億佛

功德無量

佛告阿難